KNOWLEDGE ENCYCLOPEDIA
INVENTIONS IN MOTION
INVENTIONS & DISCOVERIES

Wonder House

(An imprint of Prakash Books Pvt. Ltd.)

Wonder House Books

Corporate & Editorial Office
113-A, 1st Floor, Ansari Road,
Daryaganj, New Delhi-110002
Tel +91 11 2324 7062-65

Disclaimer: The information contained in this encyclopedia has been collated with inputs from subject experts. All information contained herein is true to the best of the Publisher's knowledge.

Printed in 2020 in India

ISBN : 9789390391271

Table of Contents

INVENTIONS THAT MOVED US

Until the Industrial Age, which began more than 250 years ago, people were dependent on animal-drawn machines for labour and travel. Oxen and mules were put to work in farms and mills, while horses pulled carriages across town and country. Travel to distant lands was largely the privilege of aristocrats, merchants and soldiers who could either afford to travel or had their travel expenses paid for by their employers.

All of this changed when human beings invented **locomotive** engines. These mechanical marvels led to a plethora of machines that could power themselves. From the basic steam engine to the powerful jet and modern electric engines, these inventions in motion are at the heart of modern ease and exploration.

A Balancing Act

The first invention that may be called a bicycle had two wheels but no pedals. It was the wooden **draisienne**, invented by a German man named Baron Karl von Drais de Sauerbrun. In 1817, he pushed and rode it for 14 kilometres, proving that it was possible to balance on two wheels while moving forward.

In 1818, some 300 modified draisiennes, called hobby-horses and **velocipedes**, were brought out by another inventor based in London called Denis Johnson. People found them expensive and difficult to use. Riders were even laughed at on the streets! Naturally, they went out of style quickly, but the idea of the cycle remained of interest to inventors. For the next 40 years, inventors created different kinds of three-wheeled and four-wheeled cycles.

◀ The draisienne was made of wood and had no pedals. The rider moved by propelling herself forward against the ground, much like Fred Flintstone in his 'car'

▲ Three-wheeled velocipedes, developed during the 1880s, were more stable than the draisienne and some could carry multiple passengers

▼ A **Victorian** couple on a **quadricycle** (four-wheeled cycle) designed for two people

⊛ Incredible Individuals

Early safety bicycles had solid rubber tyres. Though better than plain wooden tyres, these were still not very good shock absorbers. At the time, a Scottish vet by the name John Boyd Dunlop was looking to make his son's tricycle less bumpy to ride. In 1887, he got the brilliant idea of pumping air into hollow rubber tubes. He is, thus, the inventor of the **pneumatic** tyre, which is used in all bicycles today.

▲ John Boyd Dunlop speeding along on pneumatic tyres

Pedalling to Fame

The first cycle with pedals was completed by a blacksmith named Kirkpatrick Macmillan in Scotland in the 1840s. He felt that the cycle would be more usable if people could propel it forward without placing their feet on the ground.

By 1868, Europe had named velocipedes with pedals, bicycles. They were now being built out of cast iron instead of wood. Bicycles were made popular by the Olivier brothers, Rene and Aime, of France. In 1865, they pedalled a record 800 kilometres from Paris to Marseille. Their enthusiasm caught on and cycling became a popular sport among the young and the rich.

In Real Life

The penny-farthing was a boneshaker with an oversized front wheel that was better at handling bad roads. One of its riders was the world champion cyclist William 'Plugger' Martin, who won a six-day race in New York in 1891.

▲ Early bicycles like the Oliviers' had wood-spoked wheels and iron rims. They were so jarring to ride, people called them boneshakers

▲ William Walker Martin, posing with the boneshaker cycle, was the long-distance champion cyclist of the 1890s

◀ The 1885 Rover Safety was designed by John Kemp Starley. It was the first bicycle to offer true advantages in stability, braking and easy mounting

Ingenious Engines

Although we use electrical energy to power gadgets, we rarely use it to physically move objects. The prime movers in our world are engines. Most engines use either steam power or a process called internal combustion. Both types of engines are powerful technologies that came up during the 18th and 19th centuries.

▲ Invented by Hero of Alexandria in the first century CE, the aeolipile is the first known steam-driven mechanism. It is named after Aeolus, the Greek god of air

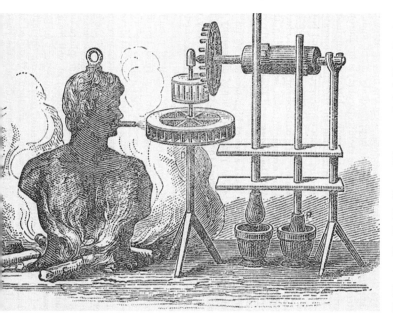

◄ Giovanni Branca's designs showed how the weight of air (steam) could be used to move gears and pistons, and thus do mechanical work. However, the method used by this machine was deemed wasteful

A Slow Start

Steam engines have been around since Hero of Alexandria built one called the aeolipile, about 2000 years ago. Unfortunately, his invention was more or less ignored as a trivial toy. Then, Taqi al-Din (in 1551) and Giovanni Branca (in 1629) described rudimentary **turbines** driven by steam power. These did not actually work on anything—they were just meant to show people how powerful steam could be.

▼ In 1802, 'Charlotte Dundas' became the first successful steamboat. She was built by William Symington

Raising Steam

The first steam engine of practical use was patented by a British inventor named Thomas Savery in 1698. The purpose was to 'raise water by fire'. It was used to raise water from underground mines. The machine worked by heating water until it turned into vapour. This vapour or steam moved to a higher container. As the steam condensed, it created a vacuum that drew up the water—similar to how you suck water through a straw. But there was little else that this steam engine could do. Also, it was a dangerous machine. The cylinder could burst in cases of excess steam! Imagine your pressure cooker blowing your kitchen to smithereens. Now imagine the havoc caused by an industrial-sized pressure chamber.

▲ A part of Savery's steam pump

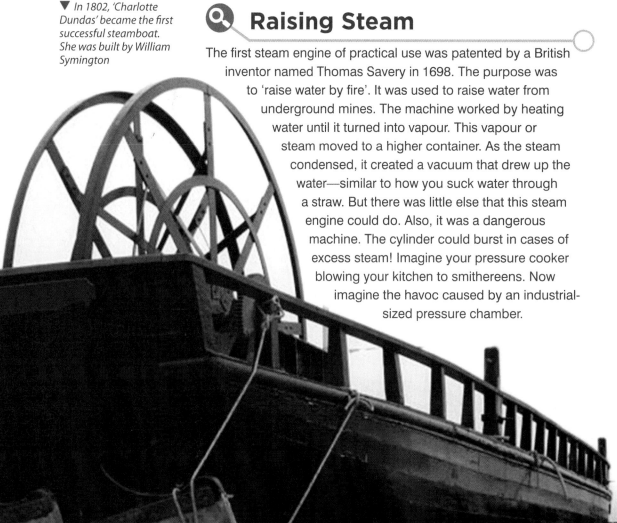

The Industrial Age Wonder

In 1712, Thomas Newcomen developed a better steam engine. James Watt further improved it in 1765. Most importantly, Watt added a rotating shaft that produced wheel-like circular movements instead of simple up-down, pump-like movements. At this point, the steam engine became immensely useful. Inventors used it to build the first locomotives (vehicles that were not pulled by animals) and kicked off the revolutionary Industrial Age!

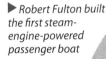

◀ *In 1803, Richard Trevithick built the first steam locomotive. It ran on a horse-drawn tram route*

▶ *Robert Fulton built the first steam-engine-powered passenger boat*

⊛ Incredible Individuals

George Stephenson, the self-educated son of a coal-mine mechanic, pioneered the railway locomotive. His steam engine was so revolutionary, the people of Stockton locked their homes and came down to see it. The Prime Minister himself travelled in it. Though famous, Stephenson was a quiet man who refused most honours offered to him, including a knighthood and a seat in the Parliament.

▲ *Stephenson's Rocket*

▼ *In 1829, engineer George Stephenson invented the railway engine. The Rocket, as it was called, became a worldwide success*

ROCKET.

What is Internal Combustion?

Combustion is simply another word for burning. Since the burning happens inside the engine, it is called internal combustion. An internal combustion engine can burn fuels such as gas, petrol or diesel to move large objects like cars and planes. There are many types of Internal Combustion Engines (ICEs), to match the many types of vehicles we use.

The Four-stroke Engine

The first successful Internal Combustion Engine was built by Belgian inventor Etienne Lenoir in 1859. It looked like a horizontal steam engine, but used an explosive mix of gases set afire by an electric spark.

The heat and pressure from the burning fuel pushed pistons and wheels, and got the machine moving. Lenoir's engine was expensive until 1878, when German inventor Nikolaus Otto added refinements that made it more reasonably available.

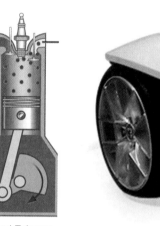
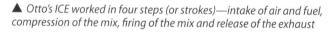

1. Intake   2. Compression   3. Fuel power   4. Fuel Exhaust

▲ *Otto's ICE worked in four steps (or strokes)—intake of air and fuel, compression of the mix, firing of the mix and release of the exhaust*

▲ *Peugeot's hydrogen-powered super car*

Isn't It Amazing!

Back in 1780, Alessandro Volta (who invented the battery) built a pistol. He did not develop it as a weapon, but rather as an experiment. In fact, it was pretty useless as a weapon.

Volta's Pistol, as it was called, used an electric spark to ignite a mix of air and fuel (hydrogen), thus using the same principle as today's car engines. Of course, pistols became much more advanced after that.

▶ *Alessandro Volta discussing electricity with Napoleon Bonaparte*

The Diesel Engine

Rudolf Diesel of Germany came across Otto's engine soon after it was invented. He set about making it more efficient and developed his 'combustion-powered engine'. In 1892, the government recognised it as the diesel engine.

Although this was truly a powerful engine, it was noisy, smelly (due to noxious exhaust fumes) and worked best at lower speeds. Over the 20th century, most countries banned diesel engines from small vehicles. Today, we see them largely in heavy goods carriers like trucks, ships and road trains.

Smaller and Faster

In 1885, Germans Gottlieb Daimler and Wilhelm Maybach famously invented an engine that resembled a grandfather clock, hence it was called the grandfather clock engine. It was the first small, high-speed ICE to run on petrol. It was the grandfather of all modern petrol engines. Daimler and Maybach fitted it on to a number of vehicles, including a cycle, a stagecoach and a boat.

Engines and Pollution

Our engines release toxic gases into the air, such as carbon dioxide—the main cause of catastrophic climate change—or sulphur dioxide and nitrogen oxides, which cause acid rain, breathing problems and ozone depletion, among other issues. Hence, it is important to use engines that are good for the environment. These engines should use less harmful fuels like hydrogen, liquefied petroleum gas (LPG) and biodiesel. Electric cars with solar-powered cells (batteries) may be the 'cleanest' engine on the horizon.

▲ Daimler and Maybach's grandfather clock engine

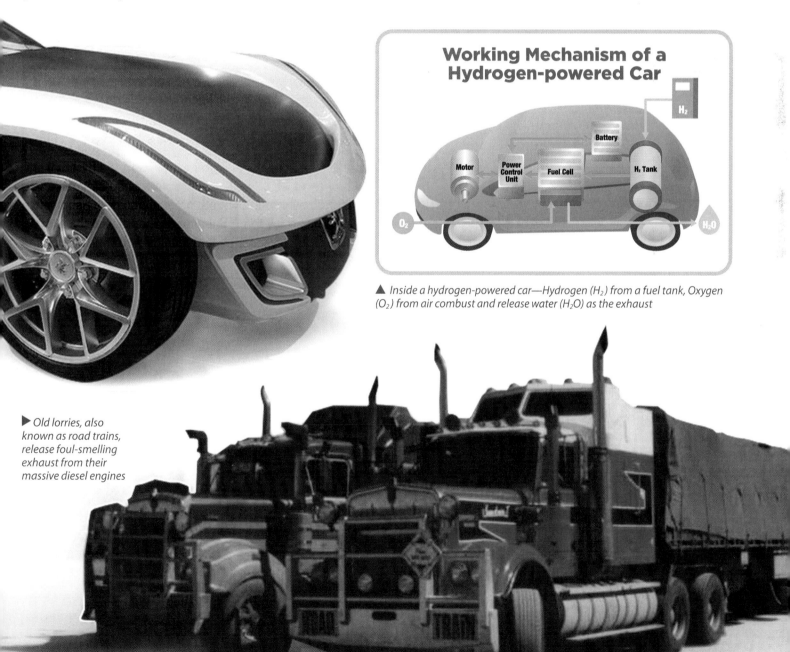

Working Mechanism of a Hydrogen-powered Car

H_2

Battery

Motor

Power Control Unit

Fuel Cell

H_2 Tank

O_2

H_2O

▲ Inside a hydrogen-powered car—Hydrogen (H_2) from a fuel tank, Oxygen (O_2) from air combust and release water (H_2O) as the exhaust

▶ Old lorries, also known as road trains, release foul-smelling exhaust from their massive diesel engines

The First Cars

In the early 20th century, nearly 80 per cent of all American cars ran on either steam or electricity. Petrol cars were noisy, shaky and often broke down. Steam cars too had many complications. In contrast, electric cars were easy to start, silent and needed little maintenance. Unfortunately, the ever-polluting petrol car squashed out its competition over time. It has dominated our roads ever since.

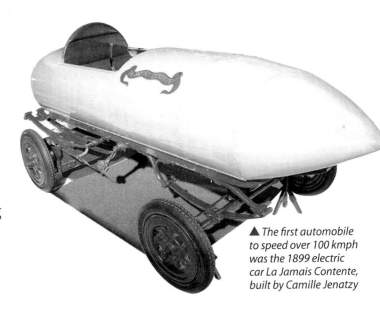

▲ *The first automobile to speed over 100 kmph was the 1899 electric car La Jamais Contente, built by Camille Jenatzy*

🔍 Karl Benz and the Petrol Car

The car is a complex creature. Its many parts are the brainchildren of different people. However, Karl Friedrich Benz of Germany is considered the inventor of the first 'true' automobile which was powered by gasoline. Called the Motorwagen, this three-wheeled car was built in 1885.

Benz also invented the **accelerator**, the battery-operated ignition, the **spark plug**, the **gear shift**, the **water radiator**, the **clutch**, the **carburettor** and the axle-pivot steering system. In 1896, he designed a high-performance engine that is still used in racing cars today!

▲ *In the Motorwagen, the passengers and the engine sat above two wheels; the front wheel steered the car*

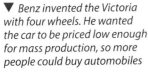

▼ *Benz invented the Victoria with four wheels. He wanted the car to be priced low enough for mass production, so more people could buy automobiles*

💡 Isn't It Amazing!

Early cars were quite different from the ones we see today. The Motorwagen of early 1888 was pushed, not driven, up sloping roads and hills. Early car owners had to buy petrol at pharmacies where it was sold as a cleaning product. Naturally, they did not have it in large supply. Interestingly, the first Benz car was bought in the summer of 1888.

◀ *The photograph shows a reconstruction of da Vinci's self-propelled cart. Renaissance genius Leonardo da Vinci designed and described an automobile way back in 1509*

In Real Life

Some countries historically banned women from driving. Locomotion has given humankind a great deal of freedom of movement, and some people wanted to withhold this freedom from women. In June 2018, Saudi Arabia became the last remaining country to lift the ridiculous ban on female drivers.

◀ *A poster from Saudi Arabia's #women2drive movement*

Incredible Individuals

The story goes that Benz's wife, Berta, once secretly took the Motorwagen to visit her mother, who lived 106 kilometres away. Berta started the drive on the morning of August 5, 1888 and brought along her sons Eugene and Richard.

On the way, she had to hunt for fuel at pharmacies and overcome numerous technical and mechanical problems. The trio finally arrived at night and sent off a telegram to Benz announcing their achievement!

The event is now celebrated every year in Germany with an antique automobile rally.

▶ *One of the official signposts along the 194-kilometre long Bertha Benz Memorial Route, in memory of 'man's' first long-distance car journey*

▲ *Henry Ford launched his famous Model T in 1908. This low-priced, easy-to-maintain car revolutionised the industry by turning cars into daily necessities; earlier, they were seen as luxury items*

▼ *France's motor industry began in 1890 with cars made by Armand Peugeot and Emile Levassor. Peugeot cars were seen at this 1901 Paris Motor Show*

Collectable Cars

Sometime over the years 1925–1928, fast luxury motorcars became status symbols. Considered to be classic cars, these are now highly valued by collectors. However, every decade since then has seen technical and mechanical advances, producing cars of greater efficiency and sheer beauty.

◀ *This 1929 Phantom belongs to Rolls Royce, whose brand is synonymous with limousines and luxury sedans*

▶ *Aston Martin, the British luxury automobile, is most famous for being James Bond's car*

🔍 Racing Cars

Car racing is one of the world's most extreme and exciting sports. Organised racing began in 1894 with an 80-kilometre race. The spirit of competition soon led to special cars being invented just for racing. The technological advancement that came forth in racing hugely benefitted the manufacture of civilian cars. It also advanced our discoveries in **aerodynamics**. In the years following WWII, Europe saw the rise of Formula One (F1) racing. Nowadays, F1 cars are some of the fastest racing cars in the world.

▼ *By the 1950s, Jaguar was building sleek and powerful sportscars like the C-type racer*

▶ *The Bugatti Type 35, one of the early cars built specifically for racing*

🔍 Breaking Speed Records

On 8 March, 1886, Daimler and Maybach secretly brought home a stagecoach, telling their neighbours it was a birthday gift for Mrs Daimler. With the help of their grandfather clock engine, they turned it into the first four-wheeled automobile to reach a speed of 16 kmph. Today, the fastest vehicle on land is the Thrust SSC. On 15 October, 1997, American Andy Green drove it at speeds faster than sound, making it a supersonic car!

▼ *Reaching a speed of 301 kmph, the Hennessy Venom GT is possibly the fastest racing car in the world*

▶ *Set up in Italy in the 1960s, Lamborghini is known today for its top-of-the-line sports cars. Like all Lamborghinis, this 2011 Aventador is named after a fighting bull*

▶ *The Thrust SSC reached speeds of 1227.985 kmph in the Black Rock Desert of Nevada, USA*

A World on Track

A train is a long string of cars (or carriages) that is pulled along by an engine. It transports either people or goods from place to place. There are many different kinds of trains, such as monorails, funiculars, turbo trains, bullet trains, double-deckers and even 'toy' trains.

▶ The toy train of Darjeeling (India) runs on narrow rails along the Himalayas. This railway is now a UNESCO World Heritage Site

▲ A double-decker hi-speed train in France

Passenger Trains

Trains that carry people over long distances are called passenger trains. They are powered by diesel engines. Faster, modern passenger trains are powered by electricity. Long-distance trains are designed to be comfortable. Their seats often double up as beds. They also have plenty of luggage space. Some passenger trains even have dining cars.

City Trains

A commuter or city train carries large numbers of people over short distances. They are most often used to travel between work and home. Commuter trains have a lot of standing space. This allows them to carry more people during each trip. Seating and luggage space are minimal. Most commuter trains run on electricity.

▲ The commuter trains of Mumbai, India, carry hundreds of thousands of passengers each day

Metros

Another way of travelling in large cities is the metro system. This consists of electrically powered trains. The tracks are underground or raised above ground. Metro trains can accelerate much faster than long-distance trains.

▲ London metro tube

Monorails

The monorail is a special type of metro. It consists of a single track (instead of two parallel rail tracks). The train straddles the track—that is, covers it from side to side. Sometimes, the track runs above the train! In such cases, the train is suspended from the track.

▲ Tokyo Monorail

Freight Trains

Freight trains are also called goods trains. These are used to transport overland cargo. Traditionally, workers would load the cargo into box wagons. Nowadays, cranes lift large containers of goods into and out of the wagons. Sometimes, trucks carrying goods drive on to the freight trains. At their destination, the trucks disembark and continue onwards by road.

▼ A freight train carrying cargo containers

To Keep the Wheels Turning

Another exciting form of transport is the motorcycle. It provides the flexibility of a bicycle along with the convenience of a car! In November 1885, Daimler installed a smaller version of the grandfather clock engine on a wooden bicycle, creating the first petrol-powered motorcycle. It was named the Reitwagen (the riding car). Daimler's partner Maybach rode it for 3 kilometres by the River Neckar, reaching speeds of 12 kmph.

◀ In 1884, Edward Butler built the first commercial motorcycle. It had three wheels and ran on petrol

🔍 Evolving Motorcycles

In the early 1900s, inventors everywhere were attaching engines to cycles and creating their own versions of the motorcycle. A lot of them were sold on the streets and were called touring machines.

In an effort to discover top-notch bikes, the first motorcycle races were set up at the Isle of Man. Of these, the 1907-established Tourist Trophy (TT) race became the most famous and most extreme form of bike racing in the world.

▲ The BAT twin-cylinder motorcycle of 1910 set a new track record of 80 kmph at the TT race

🔍 Springing to Action

Nowadays, motorcycles come in a variety of designs depending on what you need them for. People enjoy riding motorcycles for long journeys, navigating city roads, adventure biking, and racing, to name just a few.

▲ By the end of WWI, Harley Davidson was the largest motorcycle manufacturer, selling in 67 countries

⭐ Incredible Individuals

Born on 17 November, 1906, Soichiro Honda was the pioneering force behind Honda motorcycles, one of the largest motorcycle manufacturers today. Starting out as a teenage mechanic, he began inventing automobile parts during WWII. Over his lifetime, he gained recognition for over 100 inventions!

In 1945, he founded what eventually became the Honda Motor Company, which built light motorcycles that ran on small but efficient engines. By the 1980s, Honda was the third-largest Japanese automaker.

Honda himself had strong ethics. He built close relationships with his workers. He stood firm against the government when it tried to limit Japan's auto industry. And even in his 60s, he was still personally testing new models of motorcycles.

▲ Soichiro Honda

▼ Nowadays, the Japanese manufacturers Honda, Yamaha, Kawasaki and Suzuki dominate the world of motorcycles

The Omnibus Edition

The modern word 'bus' is short for the older word, 'omnibus', where the Latin 'omnis' means 'for all'. Hence, these large cars were meant for all people. Omnibuses were originally powered by horses.

The Popular Omnibus

When locomotives took off, not everyone could buy an expensive motorcar. The first motorised road-transport for the public came in the form of trams. In 1834, Thomas Davenport, an American blacksmith, found a way to drive a battery-powered car on tracks. In the 1860s, this idea was expanded into tramways that carried electrical passenger-cars on tracks.

▲ *Horse-drawn buses, called omnibuses, have been around a long time. They can still be seen in England*

From Tram to Bus

The problem with trams is that, like trains, their routes are rigidly fixed. Also, they are suitable only for smooth town or city roads. People had to use stagecoaches to travel through the countryside at the time.

In 1830, Sir Goldworthy Gurney powered a large stagecoach using a steam engine. This was likely the world's first motorbus. Petrol engines were used in buses about 60 years later, starting in Germany. Over 1905–1962 buses in Berlin actually pulled trailers to carry more passengers. Today, buses are the only feasible mode of transportation for many families who cannot afford cars or are environment-conscious.

▲ *Trams were powered by electrified wires that ran overhead along the length of the tramlines*

Modern Buses

Numerous types of buses have been invented over the years, but we recognise four main categories: the city bus, the double-decker bus, the long-distance tour bus and the school bus. The double-decker is the much-beloved giant among buses and is occasionally seen in cities. Open-roofed double-deckers are often run by tourist companies to ferry people around landmark sights in cities like London. School buses are mostly run by private companies. They follow the system of public transportation, with buses halting at a certain point where the parents come to collect their children. Long-distance buses might be private or government-run.

▶ *City buses often have low maximum speeds, two entrances and no luggage space*

◀ *A double-decker bus*

To Reap What We Sow

Farming is one of the hardest, noblest jobs on the planet; it supports billions of lives. Inventions in agriculture are therefore of great importance to humankind. Since the start of the Industrial Age some 200 odd years ago, various machines have been created to reduce the burden of work on farmers. Key among them are machines that can harvest, thresh and winnow (clean) grain-producing crops.

▲ Combine harvesters were first seen in the 1830s. For nearly 100 years, they needed horse power to operate

▲ Featured here is a steam-powered tractor. Early tractors had steel tyres with numerous projections. This helped the vehicle grip the ground and pull its load forward. Tractors with oversized rubber tyres first appeared in 1932 and rapidly became a standard feature

▼ A modern combine harvester uses different types of detachable 'heads' to meet its functions. This harvester is using a wide-mouthed reaper to harvest a field

The Combine Harvester

A working vehicle that combines all these three abilities is called a combine harvester. The earliest combine harvesters were pulled along by large teams of horses or mules—sometimes as many as 30 horses! Nowadays, harvesters run on internal combustion engines like most vehicles on the road.

To Sow, so We May Reap

The tractor is a farm vehicle with enormous rear wheels. It is used to pull heavy machinery for ploughing, planting, tilling and various such activities. Traction engines used to be powerful steam-powered machines that drew heavy loads and ploughs over rough ground. They were a modification of portable steam engines used on farms in the late 19th century. The first farm vehicle to run on a petrol-powered engine was invented in 1892 by John Froehlich, an American blacksmith. By WWI, tractors had become a common sight. In fact, the US Holt model even inspired the creation of WWI military tanks.

Optimum Agriculture

Farming has become so advanced, it even uses space technology! Specifically, farmers can now buy tractors with GPS and sophisticated computers. This allows tractors to function like drones.

For instance, using information from satellites, the vehicle is able to plough land in a precise way. There is no overlap, no missed land and no wastage of fuel.

Army on Wheels

The first armoured locomotive was built in 1900 in England. It ran on steam engines and hauled supplies during the Boer War (1899–1902) of South Africa. The first motorised weapon-carrier had been built a year earlier. This was a quadricycle mounted with a machine gun. It was not long before inventors began putting armour and motor together to create formidable vehicles for military forces across the globe.

▶ *Fredrick Simms on his gun-toting 'motor scout'*

Barrelling Through Enemy Lines

Tanks were first seen during WWI. They were deployed by the British against the Germans in September 1916. Between the two armies lay the fearsome 'no man's land' of Somme—a hellish marsh of bombed trenches, barbed wire and dying soldiers. Neither army was able to move forward. That is, until the British Mark I tanks arrived on the scene. Equipped with machine guns and running on chain-like tracks, they were able to cross the trenches and wires, and effectively support their soldiers. The clear advantage offered that day fuelled the beginning of tank warfare!

▲ *A Mark I tank in the Chimpanzee Valley on 15 September, 1916, the first day of battle for the tanks*

The Amphibious Assault Vehicle (AAV)

In 1935, engineer Donald Roebling built a lightweight aluminium vehicle that worked both in water and on land. Named the Alligator, it was used as a rescue vehicle. At the time, the US Marine Corps was looking for a tank-like vehicle to protect its soldiers during beach landings. Inspired by the Alligator, they built a powerful steel-plated version in 1941. This was the LVT (Landing Vehicle Tracked). So useful was the invention, that some 18,620 LVTs were made during WWII. Continuous improvements took place over the next few decades and other countries built their own designs. By 1985, the US had renamed it the Amphibious Assault Vehicle.

▼ *An AAV of the Assault Amphibian Battalion, 2nd Marine Division, making its way into the water, in 2011*

Smart Mobility

Modern vehicles have made the world a closely connected place. But they have also created some troubling issues. Think traffic jams, noise pollution, global warming, oil spills in the ocean, mining hazards and health concerns from air pollution.

▲ The Tesla Roadster, an electric sports car

🔍 Electric Cars

Electric cars were invented in the 19th century. They can be energy efficient; they do not create air or noise pollution; and they do not need expensive fuels like petrol. Despite this, the first mass-produced car to run on electricity was launched only in 1997. This was Japan's Toyota Prius. Since then, many automobile companies have joined the race to invent better electric cars and set up charging points, so people can 'refuel' conveniently. In addition, batteries are becoming more powerful, so cars can travel farther on a single charge, and also recharge at a faster pace.

▲ Socket for an electric car battery charger

▶ An electric car charging point in Germany

🔍 Self-driving Vehicles

Our cars are already chock-full of advanced technology for easy travel. For instance, modern cars feature satellites and GPS to help find the destination and guide the driver there on the shortest route with the least traffic. But this is just the beginning of smart vehicles.

Many automobile and technology companies are inventing cars that can function without a human driver. These self-driving (automated) cars use a mix of radar, laser, GPS and other sensors and technologies to safely navigate roads. Of course, this is not limited to cars. Delivery trucks may also soon be fully automated. In early 2018, Starsky Robotics's self-driving truck became the first of its kind to safely make an 11-kilometre journey on a public road, without a driver.

▲ We may soon have cars that can sense pedestrians and other vehicles and maintain a safe distance from them. This would greatly increase road safety

▶ Google's self-driving car

Maglev Trains

Maglev is short for magnetic levitation. The name is used for high-speed trains that move while floating over **electromagnetic** tracks. Maglevs do not have an engine. Instead, they have powerful magnets below the train. When electricity passes through the railway track (also called guideway), it becomes magnetised, and repels the magnets below the train. The reaction is so strong that the entire train is lifted just above the guideway.

If you have seen magnets, you know that like poles repel and opposite poles attract. This rule is used to create a system of power at the front of the train, causing it to move forward to its destination.

Making Maglevs

Maglev trains were first thought of by Robert Goddard and French-born engineer Emile Bachelet. The first Maglev train for public use was built in 1984–1985, in the United Kingdom, between Birmingham airport and a nearby station.

◀ The Hyperloop—a special kind of Maglev, currently under construction—travels at speeds up to 1,080 kmph inside a fully enclosed, near-vacuum tube

▼ The longest Maglev today is in Shanghai. It is 30 kilometres long and transports people from downtown Shanghai to Pudong International Airport. The system that uses magnets to repel the train from the track is called an electrodynamic suspension (EDS) system

Ships Ahoy!

Human beings have been using rowing boats since prehistoric times. The first sailboats were seen on the River Nile and belonged to the ancient Egyptians. By the Iron Age, ships were large enough to carry several tonnes of cargo between prosperous trading port cities.

Until the Industrial Age, all river and seafaring vessels, large and small, were powered either by oars or by wind sails. The speed of a sea craft is measured in knots. A speed of 1 knot means the boat is travelling at 1.8 kmph.

In Real Life

Did you know, Queen Elizabeth I of England had an official person who uncorked 'ocean bottles'? His duty was to open messages from bottles that washed ashore. This was a serious and important job! In fact, it was a capital crime for anyone else to do this, as the Queen believed that these seafaring secrets may have come from spies abroad.

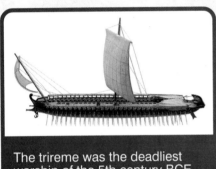

The trireme was the deadliest warship of the 5th century BCE. It needed 170 oarsmen arranged in three rows, one above the other, to propel the ship.

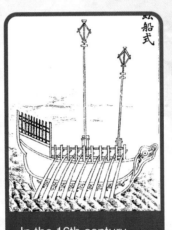

In the 16th century, the Chinese were inspired by Portuguese treasure ships to build their own galleys, called Wugongchuan (centipede ships).

All at Sea

After 1200 CE, sailing ships truly came into their own. The stern rudder was invented to guide the ship more firmly. Deep-draft hulls were successfully engineered to hold more cargo and speed across oceans.

By the 14th century, shipbuilding got so specialised that warships became separate from merchant vessels. From the 15th century onwards, ships also had multiple masts and complex arrangements of sails.

Christopher Columbus's 15th-century ship, named *Santa Maria*, was the flagship on his first voyage to the Americas.

Queen Anne's Revenge was the ship of the most famous pirate, Blackbeard.

▼ *Viking longships terrorised the European seas for more than 1500 years. During the Dark Ages, these boats carried warriors from the icy north to plunder and colonise new lands*

▶ *Mayflower— the ship that carried the pilgrims to America*

Making Waves

Steam-propelled boats were first seen during the late 1700s. Some of them worked and some did not. By the early 19th century, American inventor Robert Fulton had developed steamboats that were strong enough for commercial use. He also built the US Navy's first steam warship, the *Demologos*. These vessels moved using steam-powered paddles arranged in the form of a wheel, at the boat's side or stern. The paddle was later replaced by the screw propeller, which was more resistant to storm damage and easier to steer with. Eventually, screw propellers were combined with steam-turbine engines, as seen in modern steamships. By WWI, coal and oil were also being used as fuel.

The famous *Titanic* was powered by multistage steam turbines, an 1894 invention of Sir Charles Algernon Parsons, who first used them in the yacht *Turbina*.

The 19th-century paddle steamer, *Queen Victoria*.

The 1843-built *Great Britain* was the first ship to have a full iron hull. Iron-clad warships were extensively used in the American Civil War (1861–1865).

Military Matters

During WWII—and even after it—a great number of ships were constructed with ever-advancing technology. Such vessels served naval forces both as warships and cargo vessels. Many technologies made their way into luxury cruisers and merchant ships. While steam engines continued to run passenger ships, diesel and oil engines became popular for freighters. Earlier inventions such as radars also went through refinements.

▲ In 1910, the USS Birmingham became the first ship to launch an aeroplane. Eight years later, HMS Argus became the first true aircraft carrier that could transport, launch and land aeroplanes

Radar

Radar is a type of active electromagnetic sensor. It is used for finding, identifying and tracking objects that are far away. The objects are usually air or sea crafts and weapons. The radar works by sending out electromagnetic waves through the air and listening for any echoes that come back. The waves sent out are usually microwaves, which are very similar to what heats your food at home.

Oil tankers are the behemoths of the ocean. This supertanker can carry 2 million barrels of crude oil.

Under the Sea

Submarines are closed ships that move both on and under water. They were first used as weapons during the American War of Independence (1775–1783). But it was only in WWI, when Germany used them to fire torpedoes at merchant ships, that submarines acquired a fearsome image. The modern nuclear-powered submarines first appeared in the 1960s. They are able to stay underwater for several months at a time and are armed with some of the deadliest weapons known to humankind.

Early Submarines

British mathematician William Bourne was the first to seriously think about an underwater ship or a submarine. In 1578, he wrote of an enclosed, waterproof boat that could dive beneath water and row through it.

The first person to build such a machine was Dutch inventor Cornelius van Drebel. Over 1620–1624, he tried out his vessel in the River Thames. So successful were his trials, even King James I of England went into his submarine for a short ride!

◀ *In 1800–1801, steamboat inventor Robert Fulton built a submarine called Nautilus for Napoleon Bonaparte. Made from copper and iron, it held enough air to support four men and two burning candles for three hours*

In Deep Waters

In the late 1800s, submarines became more powerful with the help of steam turbine engines and internal combustion engines. The first submarine ever to run on a battery-powered motor was called *Nautilus* (not to be confused with Fulton's machine). Germany's infamous U-boats (from the German word *Unterseeboot*) were the terror of WWI. The U-1 was built in 1905. It revolutionised the way submarines worked. The machine used a diesel engine to move on water, but a battery to move under water. This became the standard for submarines until the end of WWII.

In Real Life

The first military submarine, the *Turtle*, was built by American inventor David Bushnell in 1775. Though it was meant to take down British warships, none of its missions were successful.

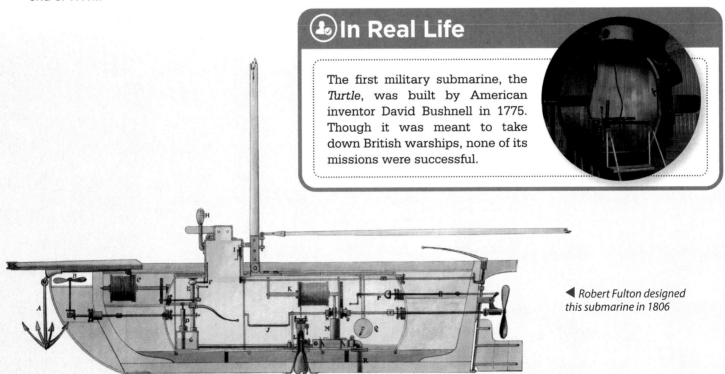

◀ *Robert Fulton designed this submarine in 1806*

Nuclear Submarines

The problem with the diesel-electric engine was that a full battery lasted no more than two hours at top speed. This severely limited the usefulness of submarines against the more powerful surface carriers and warships. This changed with the invention of yet another *Nautilus* in 1954, which became the first nuclear-reactor powered submarine. Invented in the US, it needed only a very small amount of a nuclear fuel called uranium. But with this small quantity, it could stay underwater and move at high speeds for as long as needed. Amazingly, the speed was still created by steam-driven turbines, only the fuel was no longer oil, coal or electric battery.

▲ *Modern model of a submarine. These kinds of submarines are used by nations around the world*

▶ *Built in 1940, the V-80 used a turbine engine invented by German scientist Hellmuth Walter. It burned hydrogen peroxide (used in disinfectants and bleaches). This released oxygen (instead of steam) that propelled a turbine and powered the submarine*

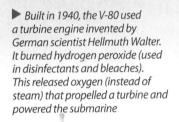

⭐ Incredible Individuals

German inventor Wilhelm Bauer (1822–1875) was a pioneer submarine-builder. During the coronation of Russia's Tsar Alexander II, Bauer took several musicians into his submarine at St Petersburg's Kronshtadt harbour. Once under water, they began playing the Russian national anthem, which was heard by people in ships across the harbour! Bauer's 52-foot iron submarine *The Marine Devil (Le Diable-Marin)* could carry 11 people and had windows, from which Bauer took what may be the world's first underwater photographs.

▲ *Coronation of Alexander II by Mihaly Zichy*

▼ *Gato- and Balao-class submarines were used in the US submarine campaign during the Pacific war*

Flights of Fantasy

Human beings have wanted to fly like birds since time immemorial. Our myths and legends are full of heroes who found ways to fly, like Icarus of Greece who flew too close to the Sun on wings of wax and feathers, or King Kaj Kaoos of Persia who harnessed eagles to his throne and flew over his kingdom. Even so real a figure as Alexander the Great is mythologised as flying in a basket pulled by gryphons!

A Timeline of Flight

The first person to design realistic flight was Leonardo da Vinci. In the late 15th century, he illustrated his theories of flight with the ornithopter. Since then, flying has come a long way.

Isn't It Amazing!

The modern conception of the aeroplane dates as far back as 1799. The concept was another of Sir George Cayley's achievements.

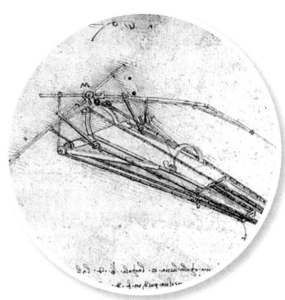

▶ The ornithopter was never actually built, but da Vinci's concept can be seen in modern-day helicopters

1783

The brothers Joseph and Jacques Montgolfier invent the first hot-air balloon. Its first live passengers are a sheep, a rooster and a duck. A few months later, Pilatre de Rozier and Francois Laurent are its first human passengers.

▲ Crowds watch the Montgolfier Balloon ascend from the Royal Estate of Aranjuez, Spain

1804

English engineer Sir George Cayley successfully flies a model glider. In 1853, he sends his frightened coachman on the first manned glider flight!

▲ George Cayley's glider

Incredible Individuals

Amelia Earhart is one of the most inspiring aviators of all time. Even as a child, she was independent and adventurous. Earhart fell in love with flying in the 1920s. In 1928, she became the first woman to fly across the Atlantic Ocean. In 1931, she set the record for highest altitude reached in flight.

Throughout her life, Earhart's exploits captured the public's imagination. On 1 June, 1937, she set off to fly around the world. Until 2nd July, she was recorded making regular fuel stops. But she was never seen again, after that day. A massive rescue party—the most expensive in American history until then—was launched to find her. It did not turn up any clues. On 5 January, 1939, Earhart was declared dead. An eternal celebrity, Amelia Earhart is the subject of many books, movies and plays.

▲ Amelia Earhart, one year before her fateful journey

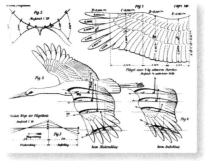

◀ Drawings from Lilienthal's book titled Bird Flight As The Basis Of Aviation

1891

American scientist Samuel Langley successfully builds a model plane powered by a steam engine. However, when he tries to convert it into a full-sized plane, it turns out to be too heavy and crashes to the ground.

1896

After more than 2500 flights, German engineer Otto Lilienthal is unfortunately killed in 1896, when his glider crashes due to strong winds. Lilienthal's pioneering book on aerodynamics is later used by the Wright brothers for their designs.

▲ Otto Lilienthal (1848–1896)

1903

The Flyer, built by brothers Orville and Wilbur Wright, lifts off at 10:35 am on 17th December. It weighs about 272 kilograms and is piloted by Orville. The brothers take turns to fly it. During the first flight that day, the Flyer covers about 120 feet in only 12 seconds.

▶ Markers at the Wright Brothers National Monument

END OF 1ST FLIGHT
TIME: 12 SECONDS
DISTANCE: 120 FT
DEC. 17. 1903
PILOT: ORVILLE

Soaring High

The Wright brothers' Flyer is a biplane. This is a flying machine with two sets of wings, one above the other. Throughout WWI, this was the most popular model for planes. From the 1930s onwards, advancements such as stronger engines and better building materials led to improvements in the monoplane. These became the regular aeroplanes we see today. The conquest of the skies gave some countries a huge advantage over others. Over the 20th and 21st centuries, it led to fierce technological competition, which has given us some truly advanced planes.

▶ *The jet engine was invented around 1936–1937 in Great Britain, by Frank Whittle, and in Germany by Hans von Ohain. In 1939, the German-made Heinkel He 178 became the first jet plane*

▲ *One of the earliest iconic plane chases belongs to Alfred Hitchcock's suspense thriller North by Northwest, where actor Cary Grant is chased by a crop duster*

🔍 Crop Dusters

After WWI, people began to use old biplanes to fly over farms and spray pesticides. This process, called crop dusting, is still in use today—though not with biplanes anymore.

Manfred von Richthofen, or 'the Red Baron' was possibly Germany's top flying ace during WWI. He shot down some 80 enemy aircrafts, many of them from a German Fokker, which was a triplane. The Baron himself was killed while flying this plane on 21 April, 1918.

▲ *The largest airship ever built was the 245-metre-long German* **zeppelin**, *Hindenberg, which could carry over 1,000 people. In 1937, its hydrogen-filled balloon caught fire and crashed, killing 36 people. This marked the end of commercial zeppelins*

💡 Isn't It Amazing!

On 14 October, 2012, Felix Baumgartner jumped off a capsule on the edge of space (38.9 kilometres high) with nothing to save him but a parachute. He became the first man to break the speed of sound in a free fall. His nail-biting nine-minute journey was watched that day by eight million people on YouTube!

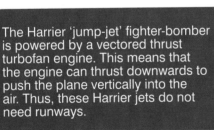

The Harrier 'jump-jet' fighter-bomber is powered by a vectored thrust turbofan engine. This means that the engine can thrust downwards to push the plane vertically into the air. Thus, these Harrier jets do not need runways.

▼ *On 14 October, 1947, the Bell X-1 became the first aircraft to exceed the speed of sound, reaching 1,126 kmph (or Mach 1.06). It was powered by a rocket engine and piloted by Captain Charles Yeager over the Mojave Desert, USA*

▲ *Felix Baumgartner*

🔍 Supersonic Passengers

The Concorde was the first commercial plane to travel faster than the speed of sound, reaching top speeds of 2,179 kmph (**Mach** 2.04). It started flying in the 1970s but turned out to be so noisy and expensive, it was shut down in 2003.

▼ *The sleek Concorde*

🔍 Around the World in Nine Days

In 1986, the Voyager became the first plane to fly non-stop around the world. Piloted by Dick Rutan and Jeana Yeager, the super-light aircraft was actually made using layers of carbon-fibre tape glued together and epoxy-saturated paper.

▲ *Almost all parts of the Voyager's frame, including the wings, were filled with fuel which was four times heavier than the plane itself*

🔍 When Cars Fly

The incredible Terrafugia Transition is a flying car! This small plane can fold up its wings in less than 30 seconds and turn into a car. It can then continue on the road and drive up to a regular petrol station if it needs to refuel. It is not yet on sale, as engineers continue to improve its technology.

The Transition can fly at speeds of 172 kmph and drive at a speed of 105 kmph. Do you think it will bring traffic jams to an end?

👤 In Real Life

After 1969, international air travel became affordable with the invention and introduction of the Boeing 747. This was the first jet plane to have a wide body, seat 400 passengers, and still fly safely and speedily across large distances.

▲ *Any plane carrying the President of the USA is called Air Force One. Since 1991, this name has belonged to a pair of specially outfitted Boeing 747 jets*

🔍 Environment-friendly Planes

Modern planes are among the biggest gas guzzlers harming our planet. In 2003, Swiss pilot and engineer Adre Borschberg began the project Solar Impulse. Its aim was to develop a plane that ran on clean, renewable solar energy. This led to the invention of the Solar Impulse II in 2014. Running entirely on batteries powered by sunlight, it circumnavigated the globe in 2016. The non-stop flight was 118 hours long—that is almost five days!

▶ *The Solar Impulse II in its hangar at Hawaii*

The Rocket Launch

The invention of the rocket engine kicked off the exploration of the vast, mysterious universe. This remarkable engine is not the creation of any one person; rather, it came about over centuries through the hard work of many scientists. Notably, in the 17th century, Sir Isaac Newton gave us the three laws of motion, which form the basis for modern rocketry. Another key figure is Robert H. Goddard, whose lifelong research in rocketry led to many innovations. Among other things, he was the first person to use liquid fuel successfully to fly a rocket.

▶ *Newton's third law says that to every action there is an equal and opposite reaction. Rocket engines act by forcing hot gases downwards. This creates an equal force in the opposite direction, which causes the rocket to shoot upwards*

🔍 The Making of Missiles

Thought to be a Chinese idea, rockets themselves were first used as weapons several hundred years back. In 1232, flaming rockets destroyed a Mongol army besieging the Chinese city of Kaifeng. These missiles were most likely made of explosive gunpowder—another Chinese invention. In Europe, rockets were first used by Mongol raiders against an army of Christian knights at the 1241 Battle of Legnica, in Poland.

⭐ Incredible Individuals

As a 16-year-old, Robert Goddard read HG Wells's thrilling science-fiction novel *The War of the Worlds*. It inspired Goddard so much, he actually dreamed of building a machine that could fly to space. On 19 October 1899, he climbed a tree behind his house and "imagined how wonderful it would be to make some device which had even the possibility of ascending to Mars..." In his diary, he wrote, "Existence at last seemed very purposive." Today, Robert Goddard is considered the father of modern rocketry.

▲ *Duke Henry the Pious led 30,000 soldiers against Mongol raiders at the Battle of Legnica. He lost to a storm of Mongol arrows and rockets*

▶ *Goddard with his first rocket*

Missile Revival

Despite its initial success, the rocket missile was more or less forgotten by the 17th century. It was revived again in 18th-century India by Hyder Ali, the ruler of Mysore. His rockets were made of metal cylinders, which could harness the power of the rocket and travel well over a kilometre. His son, Tipu Sultan used them successfully against the British in the famous battles at Shrirangapattana. This technology caught European interest and led to many rocket-propelled missiles being developed during the two World Wars. Over the 20th century, a number of other inventions were combined with rocket technology to give us the extremely sophisticated missiles of modern times.

▲ Tipu Sultan, the Tiger of Mysore, had 5,000 rocket troops in his army. Their gunpowder came from Calcutta, which had one of the largest gunpowder factories of its time

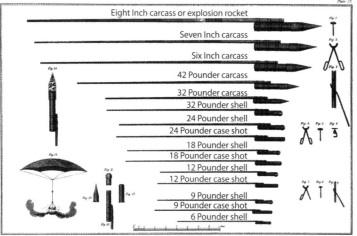

◄ Inspired by the rockets of Mysore, Englishman William Congreve experimented and designed better rockets, which were used in 19th-century warfare

An Accurate Missile

After Congreve's metal rockets, the next 19th-century innovation in rocket technology came with British engineer William Hale's invention, the rotary rocket. This used jet vents to create spin, which made the rockets more stable and accurate—much like a bullet from a modern gun.

Getting off the Ground

If an object wants to escape Earth's gravity, it needs to shoot upwards at a speed exceeding 11.2 kmph. This is called escape velocity. During WWII, the Germans built the V2 missile, which became the first rocket capable of reaching space. After WWII, the Americans acquired the V2, fitted it with instruments and sent it to space. The rocket gave us the first real data about Earth's atmosphere.

▼ The V2 rocket was designed by Werner von Braun, a controversial pioneer of the Space Age

Reaching for the Stars

Space is a scary, unpredictable place for us earthlings. Things we take for granted, like sunlight, heat, gravity, atmosphere, sound and water are out there, but in warped and extreme forms.

Space science is still new and we are still discovering the rules of this alien environment. Institutes like NASA have large teams of scientists who work together to explore our universe. Some of their most basic research involves moving about in space. After all, if we cannot move, how will we ever begin our journey?

▲ *Yuri Gagarin, the first man to walk in space*

Man-made Satellites

Launched on 4 October, 1957, Sputnik-1 was the first spaceship to successfully orbit the Earth. It moved on an elliptical path, completing its orbit every 96 minutes. In early 1952, it fell back towards Earth and burned up in the atmosphere. A month after Sputnik-1's launch, Sputnik-2 shot into space carrying the dog Laika, the first living creature to orbit the Earth.

◄ *Sputnik-1 was a little smaller than a basketball but weighed as much as an adult man*

In Real Life

On 16 July, 1969, the Apollo 11 space vehicle was launched on the Saturn V rocket. Once in space, the lunar landing module—carrying astronauts Neil Armstrong and Edwin "Buzz" Aldrin—broke away and made the first successful trip to the Moon.

Zero Gravity, Zero Atmosphere

On Earth, we are able to move by interacting with forces like gravity and air pressure. Space, however, is a near-vacuum. You can float weightlessly in it, but moving with precision is difficult. Large crafts can move using the rocket engine to thrust forward. But there is only so much rocket fuel you can carry into space.

The rocket engine is simply not fast enough to cover the enormous distances of our solar system—let alone our galaxy or the universe! Scientists are inventing new engines to solve this problem. Nuclear reactors and engines powered by plasma and magnets are some of the options.

▼ *On the Moon: lunar vehicles of a NASA expedition*

🔍 A Guide to Space Travel

The light year measures distance, not time. Light travels 3,00,000 kilometres in one second. This means, it travels 9.5 trillion kilometres in one year. This distance is called one light year. The closest stars to our Sun are Alpha Centauri A and Alpha Centauri B. They are about 4.3 light years from Earth.

The truly far-flung parts of the universe are measured in parsecs. One parsec is equal to 3.26 light years. Our galaxy, the Milky Way, is about 30 kilo-parsecs (1,00,000 light years) wide. The farthest star known to us is Icarus; it is about 15,330 mega-parsecs (50 billion light years) away.

▲ *Distances within our solar system are measured in Astronomical Units (AU). 1 AU is 14,95,98,000 kilometres. This is the average distance between the Sun and Earth. The outermost planet, Neptune is 30.1 AU from the Sun*

▲ *On 5 August, 2011, the spaceship Juno began a journey to Jupiter, reaching five years later in July 2016*

▲ *Six years after it was launched, New Horizons flew to the edge of our solar system in July 2015, becoming the first spacecraft to explore Pluto and its five moons up close*

🔍 Space Stations

Another way to overcome the problem of moving through space is to build space stations that can refuel spaceships. Since 1971, some 11 space stations have successfully orbited our planet, most famously the International Space Station (ISS). Since 1981, scientists have also launched reusable crafts called space shuttles, some of which were used to build the ISS.

▼ *People have lived on the International Space Station since November 2000. It is as big as a house with five bedrooms, and even has two bathrooms, a gym and work spaces*

Word Check

Accelerator: In a car, the accelerator is a pedal at the feet of the driver. Pressing it makes the car go faster.

Aerodynamics: It is the study of motion in air, and of the forces acting upon flying bodies.

Aviator: It is the operator (or pilot) of an aircraft.

Carburettor: It is the part of the engine where fuel and air combine and burn. The carburettor also controls the flow of air into the engine and the engine's speed.

Clutch: It is the part that connects the engine to the wheels.

Combustion: It is the process by which something is burned up.

Electromagnet: It is a magnet where the magnetic force exerted, or the magnetic field produced, is powered by electric current.

Gear shift: In vehicles, gears are used to manage speed and direction with maximum efficiency. A gear shift is the mechanism by which a driver can change gears to change speed or direction.

Locomotive: It is a big vehicle used for pulling trains.

Mach: It is a relative measurement of high speed, usually compared with the speed of sound.

NASA: The abbreviation for National Aeronautics and Space Administration, an agency that handles the USA's space research and programme

Pneumatic: In mechanics, this refers to an object that can be filled with air, or a system that works using air pressure.

Quadricycle: It is a cycle with four wheels.

Spark plug: It is a battery-operated gadget that sparks when a current runs through it. This provides the combustion for the engine.

Velocipede: It is a vehicle that runs on land with the force or effort exerted by human beings. The modern bicycle is a common example of a velocipede.

Victorian: It refers to an event, person or invention from the Victorian Era or the period during which Queen Victoria ruled over the United Kingdom.

Turbine: It is a rotating engine made using a series of curved metal plates. It moves when hit by the pressure of steam, air or water.

Water radiator: It is a cooling system that keeps the engine from overheating.

Zeppelin: It is an airship that is powered by a gigantic, bullet-shaped chamber of gas. It is named after Count Ferdinand von Zeppelin who first developed this type of airship.